T0165936

Dementia, My Darling

DEMENTIA,
MY DARLING

poems

BRENDAN CONSTANTINE

RED HEN PRESS | PASADENA, CA

Dementia, My Darling
Copyright © 2016 by Brendan Constantine
All Rights Reserved

No part of this book may be used or reproduced in any manner whatsoever without the prior written permission of both the publisher and the copyright owner.

Book layout by Keaton Maddox & Latina Vidolova
Cover artwork: *la nebbia di settembre* by Francesco Sgroi & *Emperor Gum Moth* by Fir0002

Library of Congress Cataloging-in-Publication Data

Names: Constantine, Brendan, author.
Title: Dementia, my darling : poems / Brendan Constantine.
Description: Pasadena, CA : Red Hen Press, [2016]
Identifiers: LCCN 2015050367 | ISBN 9781597097185 (paperback)
Subjects: | BISAC: POETRY / General. | PSYCHOLOGY / Mental Health.
Classification: LCC PS3603.O5579 A6 2016 | DDC 811/.6—dc23
LC record available at http://lccn.loc.gov/2015050367

The National Endowment for the Arts, the Los Angeles County Arts Commission, the Los Angeles Department of Cultural Affairs, the Dwight Stuart Youth Fund, the Pasadena Arts & Culture Commission and the City of Pasadena Cultural Affairs Division, the Ahmanson Foundation, and Sony Pictures Entertainment partially support Red Hen Press.

First Edition
Published by Red Hen Press
www.redhen.org

Acknowldgements

The author gratefully acknowledges the publishers of periodicals in which some of these poems first appeared:

Abyss & Apex: "The Winds Now;" *The Beloit Poetry Journal*: "In the Ear of Our Lord" and "The Long While"; *Academy of American Poets 'Poem A Day'*: "The Needs of the Many"; *The Bicycle Review*: "The Dreams of Trains"; *Bombay Gin*: "Pest in Blur"; *Booth*: "A Foundry Gone" and "Night Stand"; *Blueshift Journal*: "Inconsolation"; *Chaparral*: "The Man in the Next Bed"; *The Cortland Review*: "The Main Event," "The Man Who Did the Honors"; *Dash*: "En Route," "PHOTOTAXIS (No. 2)," and "Ten Alternatives to Diagnosis"; *Drunk In A Midnight Choir*: "The Guest Speaker" and "So They Keep Still"; *Easy Street*: "Dementia, My Darling" and "The War on Drugs"; *Edgar Allan Poet*: "'You Went Down to the River"; *Fogged Clarity*: "The Ultra Sound"; *Frying Pan News*: "No One Spoke"; *Ghost Town*: "All Fathers Eve," "The last thing I want to do is hurt you," and "Somniloquy"; *Hotel Amerika*: "The Class Room" and "Latitude 42"; *LUX*: "Ghost Madrigal"; *Muzzle*: "Cellar Door"; *Poemeleon*: "Poem Made Frome Letters Written By FrancEye"; *Red Headed Stepchild*: "Because You Watched *The Space Children*" and "Smiling Back"; *Runes*: "Hearth Rob"; *Salamander*: "Rule"; *Virginia Quarterly Review*: "Still Life on Mars" and "They Left Their Dog and a Record Playing"; *Wherewithall*: "PHOTOTAXIS (No.1)" and "Cinch"; *Zyzzyva*: "The Bear Chapter."

In memory of memory

Contents

Phase II: BOOK OF THE MO TH

Phase III: BEST CELLAR

Rule

for Wanda Coleman

If you break enough
lines, eventually
you have something
that'll kindle & catch
like a tar paper shack
or a wedding dress.
A long gone woman
once took a stone to
all her words until
her tongue flared
like a map of war.
A library stands
where she's buried
& people leave gifts
in the parking lot—
rock, paper, scissors.

Phase I

BLURB

"MOTH EATEN"—age-old, ancient, antediluvian antiquated, archaic, been around, creaky, dated, decayed, decrepit, dilapidated, elderly, forgotten, getting on, gray, infirm, moribund, old fashioned, outdated, passé, ragged, senescent, senior citizen, shot, tattered, threadbare, timeworn, venerable, worn, worn-out, worse for wear

GHOST MADRIGAL

Girls walk together down the leaf brown street
in time to some song they know. They walk
into winter like a neighborhood.

The song's about love, how they wait for it
to call, come dancing. There's also a lyric
about the length of night. The words

are hard to follow; the girls are laughing now
because the song is so silly or innocent or old.
It's cold, their laughter breaks behind them.

They must live around here. Or they're ghosts
and they used to. Only the dead are
so brazen, so used to a place. One waves

to a face in a passing car. It doesn't stop.
Ghosts they are. What of the leaves, the street,
the cones of orange light that pulse

as the girl go? What of it. Come dancing,
my love, come dancing. The night is too long
without dancing.

The last thing I want to do is hurt you

Before that, my love,   long before that,
I'd like to learn another language,   maybe

Portuguese   though people tell me Hindi
& Mandarin are the future,   the tongues

of men on the moon   Which reminds me,
before I hurt you   I want to go to space

& float like   a wing   What do you think
happens to birds in zero gravity;   do they panic

or relax,   finally relax   Do they become
fish   Someone must know   by now,

some astro or cosmonaut, who said,   mostly
to himself,   Don't be afraid,   I just want

to know if you can live   without doing
what you must   The last thing I want to do

is hurt you,   after I see the Grand Canyon,
the pyramids of Giza, the little cave at La Verna

where Saint Francis slept   & listened to God
& went   blind   First   I want to see

my home again,   my heavy home,   the break-
able life   I already know   I want to

have some visions,   too;   angels   or ghosts
or natural disasters   I want to warn the village,

any village,   the dam is breaking,   the fire
is building,   the air is filling with cows   Time

to make a list   How mad will you be
if you don't swim the hundred seas,   don't dive

the sky,   never go   to the cobra show
My love,   you can take it out on me

Poem Made from Letters Written by FranceEye (1922–2009)

I believe I'm awake but who knows? I need a sheep dog
to herd me back to sleep. Foggy as I am these days,
I can't even remember—
                           does your dog ever get a chance to work?

I watched a sheep dog working once, a dog whose owner
was a woman who'd been a rodeo performer. She kept sheep
just for her dog to have something to do.

I envy your cicadas. My night sounds are someone's TV
some rooms away & a neighbor yelling. Not sure
if it's male or female but the yell usually starts out,
                                                      WATER,

then a mispronounced AGUA (AGH-WA). It progresses
through NURSE to various nurse's names. Right now
it's on DEBRA!

                    I'll have to ask my friend who works tending
mentally challenged adults, if he couldn't use a sheep dog
in his work. Wouldn't that make for pleasing scenes?

Of late I have found myself nostalgic for the days of ice
and horse turds by the curb. My mother allowed us to suck
the ice, saying that the dirt melted off.
                                          Never mind,

soon I'll be elsewhere, in all probability a better "where,"
though I'll miss the woman who runs this place.
                                                 She walks
around all day in sockless shoes & rolled-up pant legs,
watching everything, & everything runs like clockwork.

Dementia, My Darling

(Poem made from lines spoken by my mother)

If someone finds me on the road
If someone finds me on the road
in my nightgown, barefoot and talking

in my nightgown, barefoot and talking
If my talking nightgown
      finds the road   in me
          and someone on barefoot

      Or I'm throwing my money to the cars
    Or I'm throwing my money to the cars
convinced I'm just feeding the ducks

convinced I'm just feeding the ducks
    I'm feeding the money,
        the cars, or the ducks,
            I'm just convinced to throwing

            Please lock me away
              Please lock me away
                and live your life

              and live your life
            and lock your life away
          Please live me

If my talking convinced someone,
my barefoot lock on the road, ducks
in the cars throwing money to live

and the feeding finds me
and I'm me
or I'm your life
please just nightgown away

FUGUE STATE

The county of Amnesia fades   a little house each day;
one of us remembers a name   and takes off
our sweater.
                    The soup's gone cold,   we blow on it
anyway, ask again,   Is this the kind with words in it?

At the Town Hall there're plenty of agendas,   hands
raised to speak,   but when our turn comes,   we yield
our time
              to whoever's still crying.   Someone's always
crying. There's a woman so old   she almost remembers

when the land was all sheep,   her father   nosing
a Model-A between them,   the shepherd walking
with the window,   saying,   Nothing for you here.
Nothing.
              Did her father really buy two sheep   without
slowing down?   Did she get to name them   something
& something else?
                          We don't record this stuff, there's no
archive; just a big map of the world   hung by a red pin
in the Arctic sea. We like to look at it,   that bright point
of no place.   We're pretty sure we've been there.

"You Went Down to the River"

The river took you, so we blamed the river.
We pointed with our phones, said, That's it,
that's the river. Naked, the police came
to pat it down, read its rights. The river ran.
We took pictures and followed fast, all but
the barefoot police, who winced and tiptoed.
The river failed the polygraph test, every
way it could: laughed, babbled, changed
its answers. What did Inconclusive mean,
we wanted to know, if not Guilty. The judge
was a painting of mountains and we cheered
because we knew he would hang. We wanted
justice like we wanted Heaven. We wanted
Heaven like we wanted new phones. We didn't
count on a jury of stones; smooth, smooth
stones. Geology says a verdict may take years,
piles of years; we should find a way to pass
the time. We go to the river, sit by the river,
hold hands by the river and sing, but not
of you; there're no good songs about you.

LATITUDE 42

Before this you were on a train, you sat
with your legs crossed, a magazine open
to a picture of lips, a neck, maybe hands

You let go and the pages turned some
easier way   A light was crossing
the window—the older shout of a candle,

not a bulb—slow because it was far away
You didn't wonder who could live there,
or wonder long; if nowhere had a middle,

it was on a train   Wave, you thought
too late   Just your face in the glass again,
wreathed; you looked you in the eye

and waited to say things you wouldn't see
coming   It happened, one of you broke,
the other got off the train

Hearth Rob

Who took away the mosque-
shaped clock that was here?
And the porcelain cumquats,
where are they?   Gone
with father's Lindberg Baby
chafing dish, no doubt.

I remember closing the door
before we went upstairs, now
it's open. Look, there are wet
leaves pressed into the rug,
someone must have come in
while we gave each other
our injections.

How did we not hear? What
else was taken? Why do so
many cures smell like new
office buildings? I tell you,
we should search this house,
cellar to weathervane.

If we find thieves, we'll take
back what's ours. If we find
no thieves, we'll make a list
of all we have yet to lose
and get busy yearning.

Pest in Blur

There's a fly in the eye

on the grandmother clock,

by the door. And when I say

an ink blot with wings,

that sings a thin hymn

by the door. When I say

a coat that goes to the floor,

unbuttoned, ajar, no body

home I mean the same thing as

from the eye to the belly

then down off the face

the negative space

and its grandmother knock

And when I say face, place,

the same thing as before,

of the black number eight

(itself a tall eight),

fly I mean

a blood spot

for the fruit we forgot

door I mean

pockets deep as tar,

home (And when I say

a jar). The fly moves

of the black number eight,

to the pendulum place,

of the clock,

by the door.

or space I mean

half of an apple

gone black in the sun,   that swelters with flies,

so wrong in the mouth,   so hard on the eyes.

Exam

Anyone who needs to see a doctor, please
stand in this line. Anyone who needs to hear
a doctor, please stand in this other line.

If you wish to feel a doctor without otherwise
engaging, remain calm, the doctor is with you.
If you dream of doctors, please wait outside

until your name is almost called. If you dream
you're a bird, please wait inside until your call
is named. If you believe the word Doctor

is a verb, run away, run away. If you believe
doctors live in white houses over white lawns
in neighborhoods of sky, please form two lines:

one on this side of the fountain,
one on this side of the fountain.

Anyone newly born or elderly, please keep to
the middle of the group. If you don't know why
you're here, think no one sees you, that you can
hide by falling into line,
                              you have already been seen.

The Man in the Next Bed

The man in the next bed has
a habit of silver; he darkens
when not under hand.
He blames the road atlas

for bringing him here, for
counting the miles in gold.
The man in the next bed is
cast out of bronze. The man

next to him out of wax. Hold
him too long, he'll furrow
and tantrum all night like
a candle. The man next to him

talks to his pillow. He blames it
for his dreams, his stumbling
& mumbling dreams. Why
did you show me tigers? Why

were my legs full of mud?
The man next to him has
an answer, he yells at the roof
till he's blue. It's raining

bishops & bastards, he cries
& hides his medicine cup
in his shirt. The nurses
don't bother to take it;

he'd only steal another
from the man in the next bed.
That man is the president
of Monaco, it says so

on his shoulder tattoo: I am
the president of Monaco.
In case of emergency, call
a jeweler. In the bed next to him

there's a man who keeps
breaking his fingers. God
tells him which to crack
or save. He leaves himself

one to point with, to accuse
the man in the next bed: the man
who built the hospital, who
doesn't remember building it,

whose heart plays the machine
beside him, whose eyes stay
open, empty as the next bed
& the next bed over.

Rime

You died believing snow
had come. You made us
stand at the window
to give you the blow by
blow. Your mother said it
looked like ash. Your sister,
the writer, said it was more
like a storm of Get Well
cards, torn and scattered
by invisible dogs. I don't
recall what I said, but dad
refused to play along, saying
it was just a bunch of big
moths buzzing the lamps
outside. Why do you say
it's snowing when it isn't?
You were gone by then,
but we didn't know because
your sister went on a rant
about poetic license.
A nurse came to shut us up
then noticed the monitor.
Christ, you people, she said.
We traded guilt while
doctors checked you over.
I remember looking up
in case some part of you
was still there, watching.
I'm not sure where I got that
idea or why I keep writing

what you already know.
Why say it's snowing
when it is.

No One Spoke

for at least an hour. Maybe longer. It was longer.
No one spoke, looked away, or drew attention
with their hands. A few of us opened our mouths,
a few always do. We didn't know we'd done it.
No one saw. Like losing a button. We were busy
not speaking. We had drinks, a few snacks, watched
TV with the sound off. A few of us thought about
the button, the one that says MUTE, how common
it is now. We tried to imagine it on other things,
things that don't speak but are loud: lamps, guns,
a fire truck with MUTE painted on it. It would've
looked good on us, stenciled white across our chests.
We wore dark colors, earth tones. No one calls them
dirt tones or soil. It's what we mean: mud, rot,
the heap of life. It'd be hard to sell clothes with
names like that. Hard to give them away. Maybe
if they were gifts. We'd all accept with a nod,
like we did when your picture came our way.

The Main Event

I have two friends left   who don't know
each other   Wonder if they should
meet at the funeral

Whenever my mother lost a boxing match,
she'd say   she came in second

At her wake my father   & her lover
knew each other   from art school

One painted the other nude   forty years
before   One made the other look good
One made   the other

My friends make me   think about dying,
about fights breaking out   on my grave,
policemen,   crisp,   painterly,

pulling my family apart   like brushes
I want everybody to know   everybody

We should give coffins   at birthdays
We should leave the world   with ribbon

ANOTHER NATURAL CAUSE

People die from falling out of bed—
five hundred a year—more than are
killed by tigers, sharks, crocodiles.
There's a quota, a "stat" on a big
chart, next to famine & disease,
murder & plane crashes. Mostly
small children, the elderly, people
who can dream too hard. At least
twice as many have to explain it
to somebody else. Thousands of
relations, not to mention cops,
medics, morticians, have to say
out loud, No, really, it happens
all the time. Tonight, while we go
to school naked, get chased by bees,
discover we can fly, a few of us
pass into nothing, into bright light,
into marble stations of cloud. We
come yawning, rubbing our faces,
our faces creased by books, cups,
clocks, whatever we kept close by.

The Guest Speaker

said our hearts are not bird's nests
or loaded guns. At least they don't
have to be for us to understand
them. For years I knew mine was
actually a toy monkey wrapped in a
prayer rug. That's why it pounded so,
why its pounding was muffled. Alas,
my heart is, always has been, what
my doctor said it was: twelve ounces
of muscle, flexing seventy to eighty times
per minute without motive, fast-
ened between my lungs in a space
unmusically named the Pericardial
Cavity; deaf, preoccupied, miraculous
without anyone noticing it's the size
of my clenched fist, a Chinese pear,
a pocket dictionary.
                              The speaker
offered many examples of Eastern
poetry (Tu Fu's forests, Basho's
frog) where the phenomenal world
is phenomenal enough. Some objected
to this & there was shouting during
the Q&A: metaphor vs. medicine.
I tried to defend my dinky monkey.
Failed. Later, in my room, I got so
quiet I could hear blood. Sounds like
blood, I said, to no one, drowning
for a moment its constant Shhhhh,
so often mistaken for an ocean
or a freeway, the steady applause
while God looks at his notes.

In the Ear of Our Lord

I thought you said you loved
the coal train's horn,
         the loneliest monk
playing piano Such distinct
sounds, I had to wonder how
you knew to love them

In the beginning was the whir,
I thought you said, & the whir
was good

Didn't you say, each verse
should end on a pyramid
                    Now
the crowds are coming home
Cross our eyes & dot our lines
I could swear you said the time
was wow, the time handsome

Hark that horn, the monk's
lonely fingers, doesn't it just
break your harp
               None of us
will be re-embered

Free alas, you said, Free alas

The War on Drugs

for Ilene Waterstone

The war called at midnight, called again
at two, third time it left a message. Made
no sense; something about wagons, a palm
tree weeping, (I played it over), weeping.
Said something else about money, a ride
to the airport. The airport was closed,
was falling, the airport was crawling
with cops. Come get me, it asked,
Can you come get me? But it never said
where. It called at sunrise, then again
at noon. Left a message, half rage, half
song—You're all a bunch of cowards.
You don't care if I die (eye, eye). To hell
with all y'all.

It must've called someone else after that,
someone who answered; a month passed.
I heard it went north. I heard Mexico.
A friend (of a friend) saw it raging in Rome.
Now it's here, in this room, with the shades
drawn and the lamps on. It won't show me
its eyes, its red, red eyes, rubbed out
like the price of a gift. It's wearing
a hospital gown over jeans, a house dress,
over nothing, wearing a helmet, a rifle.
It's barefoot, sandaled, got huge black boots
with no laces, and it's sorry.

It's so sorry about things: the disappearing,
the curses and songs. No really, it wants
to surrender. Can it stay? Some of it?
Can some of it stay the night? I should
keep away from the windows, it says,
I should kill the lights. If I say no,
it will go off, it will cry or break things,
accuse me of loving it all wrong. I love it
all wrong, as a cup loves coins, a bed loves
fire, a tree loves whoever comes to eat
its last heart. When the phone rings again,
the war watches me hesitate, then grabs
the receiver. It doesn't know its own voice
on the other end. Christ, it's so loaded,
it can't tell it's lying. Okay, it says, I'll ask,
but seriously, just for one night.

And if I let it stay, it won't stay. That is,
it'll find something of mine to steal,
then find a reason to leave, before
more of it comes—in helicopters,
rubber rafts, in busses, paper bags—
comes to take the city, mother by mother,
and pawn it. What will it get for us.

Phase II

BOOK
OF THE MO TH

*There are two varieties of moth known to favor
books: Tineola Bisselliella and Hophmannophila
Pseudospretella. Ironically the Bookworm Moth, Heliothis
Zea, does not care for books, or rather,
it no longer cares for them, or it has forgotten
that it ever did.*

Uncorrected Proof

Most of the poems in this book are
missing. They've been replaced. Just
like there used to be an apartment
where your apartment is now.

The place is haunted like the word
"Now" is haunted. People died where
you live, alone, the living and dying
both. Every inch haunted by ghosts

& their ghosts. You make a nice bed,
tie a nice bow, sing a nice song, that
song you remember while cleaning
the apartment, making noises louder

than the dead saying, Excuse me.
Saying, You're gonna' wanna'
move soon. An ocean will be here
in about a thousand years. After that

a volcano, a canyon, a forest, & then
new management. But you're good
for now. It's good.

FOREWORD

Since you can't be thanked enough /
Ladies and Gentlemen / let us begin with
Pyrrharctia Isabella / the common moth /
moth of the people / commonly the masses /
the mob / the multitudes / uncommonly
the Great Unwashed / yes / there was a time
when we said so / without a wince of regret /
also known as flinching / a flexure of muscles
about the eye / brief flooding of the Lacrimal
Mucosa / commonly the tear / romantically
jewels / pearls / blue diamonds / unromantic-
ally an alibi / trump card / doctor's note / once
called an Aegrotat / a word so ugly it could
be a flower / or bird / the Great Egret / better
known as the heron / locally the Shypoke /
meaning a feeble / sickly person / easily
flushed / but one who comes back to sing /
to drink / to sleep in peril / like me / whose
common name is You / Thank You

Acknowledgments

The poem "The Unbearably Sad Guest Room" first appeared
in the winter issue of *Unbearably Sad Things*. The journal
Unbearably Sad Things has not appeared since the winter issue.
The editor of *UST* has not appeared since the publication party
at the Unbearably Sad Bar & Grill. She left an outstanding tab
of $70 and a hair clip shaped like a grand piano, (please speak
to Esteban). Back issues of *UST* still appear in the mail for
the author of "The Unbearably Sad Guest Room." There's
a stack by the door to recycle, but he forgets to take them out.
That's not true, he remembers. Whenever he comes or goes
he remembers. There's something about that walk to the trash,
the cracked flag stones, the sound of the heavy lid, makes him
want to keep walking, to carry for miles something nobody
wants, maybe stay the night with your unbearably sad family.

EXTRACT

The more you read, the more people
there are. Read long enough, a hospital
appears. A man and woman read long
into the night. When they look up,
the doctors are red, orange, yellow,
getting lighter. On the wall is a crayon
rooster. It crows so loud it can't be
heard. Here comes the good part.

INCONSOLATION

There used to be different words here,
a lawn with benches, a statue of wind.
This is where your hand would go, my
shoulder, a good laugh. We shared
a sixth sense of humor, that is,
we always knew what the dead found
funny: calendars, money, an informed
opinion. Now the birds sing like
car alarms. The bees just want out.
You can push the night around
with your tongue.   We do.
We go to the café and order a bed.
We ask for curtains, a notebook, then
blow on our cups without drinking,
blow away. Say, How long's it been?
When's it gonna' be soon? What
we wouldn't give for what we gave.
And this is when the dead start
laughing, when you and I decide
to keep waiting. Let tomorrow cool
awhile, until we're two other people.
They'll know if we're inconsolable.
They'll know how to drink lying down.

The Class Room

The name alone would make anyone
defensive, as though it's here we
learn what we deserve. No wonder
we cut names in the desks; our names,
yours, our names for each other. I
carved mine for centuries of world
history, riding the currents of wood.
I discovered the grain was the same
on the desk beside me, and the one
beside that. The wood was fake or
rather, just a picture of wood. Every
slab was an x-ray of the same tree.
I imagined, still imagine, a forest
of redwoods growing in tight rows,
their boughs hung with text books
—*Practical Algebra, 1000 Spanish
Verbs, The Brothers Karamazov*—
and a small wind turning the pages
a little too fast to read.

PHOTOTAXIS

Whatever gets between us and the sky
becomes the sky / It's how we start to
wish on the flicker in a smoke alarm /
how sometimes the bed seems hidden
under moss / We sit long after the lamps
go down / The park so dark / the moths
dive at our phones / It makes sense to
laugh down the street / The street waits
its turn / then rolls out its black receipt
for things we don't remember / We
can't read the numbers / What we owe
is somewhere behind those trees in
the wallpaper / or way the other way

DISCLAIMER

Shakespeare's clowns aren't funny / Dante's
comedy needs work / The Book of the Dead
has no blurbs /
        For that matter Hollywood
has no holly / Trust me / *The drive I driveth*
every day /
        If we all had our own talk-shows,
we could just say "awesome" for hours
& get paid /
        Every book is a children's book /
All diamonds blood diamonds / Shakespeare's
clowns aren't funny / even in a creepy way /

Dante died making disclaimers / Tutankhamun
chose his own death / with help from adults /

This we now know / In the future everyone
will be famous for fifteen dollars / The fault
in ourselves / dear brutes / we think we're stars

A Foundry Gone

Don't worry about how much you are.
Think about ants, what fits in their mouths.
Always remember the land is a roof, always.
Early reports from behind the refrigerator
say the new queen looks a lot like her father;
when she turns her head the television flickers
but nobody stops watching. Stop watching.
Start keeping a record of everything you say
in your sleep. Translate all Freudian slips.
Sorry, that should be, "Stop begging for things."
Pavlovian slip.   Ring a bell?
Insects aren't submissive, they don't look up.
The queen is served by her masters. The land
moves fast but the dead move faster. Most
people die with ten pounds of undigested
literature in their systems. Mostly "coverage."
Ants can detect artificial sweetening, even
in a corpse. When angels die, every part is
useless. The sun is full of apologies. If you take
a Twinkie & bury it for sixty years, you'll have
no idea where you buried it. Everyone has
a question that can't wait. The opposite of love
isn't hate, it's a quick survey. The dreams of ants
are broken by starting cars, changing channels,
texting. Most of us have a higher profile before
birth, before the hammer strike of light. Some
day soon you'll be asked to melt your money
into a single coin. The hard part will be
choosing its face.

TEN ALTERNATIVES TO DIAGNOSIS

1. Tell lies while jumping rope

2. Sleep on a queen-sized photograph of an orchestra

3. Read your resume to a dog

4. Descend stairs in place

5. Fill your pockets with seawater & walk into a quarry

6. Pay someone to gift-wrap the rest of your money

7. Have your mail forwarded to an orphanage

8. Learn to read Braille with your cheek

9. Applaud the progress of shadows

10. Set your watch to the hour of your birth & remove the battery

OVER HERE, THIS ONE

My old high school talks in its sleep—

If a train carrying one red apple
leaves the earth at twice the speed
of light, who is Boo Radley?

It rolls over, steals all the blankets
from the present; God knows how
it grades me now.
                    It goes on—

Long ago, all the continents were
one document, double space. How
did this affect women?

I smooth its hair, breathe with it,
say, Let me make it up. I'll turn in
everything I owe.

And, at last, I mean it.   I do.

Put your hand down, it says,
You're in enough trouble.

EXTRACT

Hospital ceilings; why are they so alike,
he wonders, always white with black dots,
anti-constellations, why the conspiracy?
The woman answers thru a curtain, When
I was a girl, we were too poor for plates,
so we stole clocks from the school & ate
from their faces. He tries to imagine it;
the clocks still working, hands fighting back.
He can hear her going through a purse,
churning it. What does God do, she asks,
when He waits for a doctor. Does He pace?
No, the man says, He reads.

SOMNILOQUY

Fwait,   thisis th time
Go   yu shd go now
Yer r   mom
                yer momms comin

Doorss   too small
cantt fit   use th   swindow
                instead n
                          jump

Ss dark   dark outsside
y kin hear   mm walkin
in therre   nnn signinn

yer ma   iss singing
                in the bed

you h   need t hearr this s
shees   tellin the housse
how tt o   find youu

So They Keep Still

I knew a boy who ran away to join the circus.
That's what my dad said when I asked where
Tommy was. He wasn't happy here. He joined
the circus. How could I have missed such
an event? I imagined acrobats on elephants,
ambling down our street, wagons drawn by
zebras, maybe a ballerina on a bike, all slowing
traffic to a march. I could see Tommy step
in line, looking at his feet as I would do,
saying with each step, This is the farthest
I've been. No, this is the farthest I've been.
No, this . . . But he didn't say anything because
he didn't join the circus; his parents divorced
and sent him to Canada. My father had lied
like a father. I didn't know this for twenty
years until I spotted Tommy at an airport
on his way to Vancouver and his son. He
had his own divorce now. What do you do,
he asked? I tame lions, I said, so they keep still
when I put my head in their mouths. Tommy
thought I was kidding. So, how's business?
I told him the truth: I'm a failure; every lion
rips my head off, and parades through the city.

PHOTOTAXIS

light is nearsighted / relative to size / to purlieu / hardly the first time
you've stood like this / reading something / there's no word rare enough
to make it interesting / no explodable tranquility / maybe a moth / a big
moth / built to snuff the halo in a lantern / tell yourself not to brood
and it counts as brooding / only night sleeps and poorly / moths have
incredible hearing / tuned to the muttering of bats / they're good with
names / too / cross talk / the different porch lights on this block / they
hum along / who needs adjectives for darkness / their wings are made
of human dust / wait for the emergency plan / this is the emergency plan /
the lamps inside us are all the way up

The Ultra Sound

I put my hand on her stomach and feel
for the baby's head. Earthquake season.
After a beat, it finds my palm, nuzzles.
I sense other movements, a fumbling
in the dark of this woman. The couple
downstairs is blind and clumsy. Their
daughter is ashamed of her sight and
pretends to stumble all day. The baby
kicks twice, like its foot is caught on
a rug. Yes, like that, I think and move
my hand. Long ago, animals gathered
here, for water, for shade. Somehow I
can tell I'm over the face, the baby's
eyes are open, it's speaking. I kneel
to listen. A laugh begins in the floor.

Mum

the luna moth has no mouth /
to speak of /

the moon moth / Indian moth /
Actias Luna / has more names
than days to go

but no mouth / so it eats early /
in its nativity cup / where it is
itself a drink /

hey / it's just here to meet
someone / really / let it wait
by the wall /

at the window / in a lampshade /
dead center of the evening
news /

national tragedy of a moth /
no tongue / few friends / not
much luna / either /

even if it had / that is / even if
it could sing / like the great
singing moth /

Syntonarcha Minoralis / you'd
never find it / the luna moth
looks like ivy /

a leaf / with two drops of water /
that could be eyes / nowhere
near its eyes /

EXTRACT

There's no light left to write. She talks to him
from the window, over a shoulder, as if he were
a coat. He wants to be. His last line looks
like hair, a child's drawing of smoke. Instead
of smoking the woman has a bottle of soap
and blows bubbles from a little wand. He can
barely see the circles float away. Bats come,
bats whose eyes are useless, who know
the night is only crossed by screaming at it,
loud as a tisk, a turn of keys, no louder. She
wonders if the bubbles confuse them. Do they
think it's food? Do they fly home disheartened?
She dips her wand. He writes at the dark.

The Book of the Moth Club

who knew there was a book of the moth

club   who knew they did anything

but hang around & eat smoking jackets

or work   on their dust collections

they read like crazy   about lamps

& Edison & Edison lamps   & what

they read burns them like books   they

smoke in their dust jackets   never

discussing what they read   whether

the end's a surprise   & who died

it's not like they've nothing   to say

some detail always bugs them   in fact

they mean to speak up   next month

but by then   they've lost the plot

& beat their heads   all night

against a naked light   paging back

CINCH

Show me two fountains, I'll die
of thirst between them. I have
a hard time deciding, even which
things to neglect. Some other day,
I bought ten peaches and a girl
asked if I wanted a sack to carry
them home—actually she said,
Would you like a plastic bag, one
that'll still be here long after you
and I are soap? Or do you wanna'
hold'em to your chest and run off
like a pregnant horse from a fallen
city?—and I cried into my sleeve
because I wanted both. There used
to be a fountain where my people
drank from the mouth of a marble
lion. Some said the water was like
a roar, a long roar you could take
into your own throat and swallow.
Others said it was only the river
you'd expect to find inside any lion.
Every year a few of us drowned
in the act of choosing a side. One
morning an army stormed the town;
they found the streets empty and
the cemetery full, but for one man
standing in a plot, waving. Help,
he wailed, Do I look like a roar or
a river? The invaders fell back,
outnumbered.

They Left Their Dog
and a Record Playing

They left their dog and a record playing,
the boy and girl next door. Last night

they argued to music, like they do;
this morning only the song was home—

a dog asleep in the yard—the yellow dog,
the mortified, raving yard.

The girl wore an egg of amber on a chain
around her neck. The egg bore a black

widow spider; its hourglass brown
as bourbon; the sand run out for good,

for the whole neighborhood. How they
got so much in that little car

we'll never know. How they got so much,
they couldn't agree. It was what

they fought about. And the dog, the record
playing. The boy wore a wallet

with a chain to his belt. The wallet bore
a skull with smiling eyes, the word

"Misfits" worn away with paying. The door
is open, skull dark. We don't need to go

to know it's empty, to see the player
on its milk crate, playing the record over,

filling the house, spilling the dog outside,
like an oath, a vow left to keep itself.

EXTRACT

A man and a woman and a man and a man
and a woman and a woman and a room
in a hospital with high Victorian ceilings
and bare Freudian floors, lit by twenty-six
Abecedarian windows are all recurring
images in the coloring book of the dead.
When the rooster crows the crayons
sink down in bed. It's too early and
everyone was having a really good dream.
We were in love with the last person
we should love, only now they were first.
Doctors came, Sky Blue and Antique Brass,
Dandelion and Scarlet, to say
the weddings would go ahead as planned.
This is not to make light of the facts
but there are none. At this hour
all we know is the author-
ities cannot determine the exact cause
of tragedy. Several men and women
have come forward to identify the remains
of the day. This is the day, they say,
we'd know it anywhere. But those clothes,
the shoes and wristwatch, they must be gifts,
we've never seen them.

Cellar Door

for Jennifer Foerster

So I'm reading your book,
the part where you let go
of your imaginary friends
& I stop because mine are
suddenly back. It's terrible,
they never liked me. I didn't
remember that until now,
until you opened your hand,
they hated me. Why the hell
would I invent playmates
who stopped playing when
I approached, who sighed
when I spoke? There was
actually a day when I begged,
begged to go with them
to the cellar. They refused &
blocked the door. Forty years
they've been down there.
They look it, too; rotten
playsuits, stick bodies,
scribbles for eyes. They
squint, slow to react, slow
to guess what's next, even
when I push them into the car.

PHOTOTAXIS

Light is struck into radiance / slapped actually /
stars redden / turn away / I sleep through it /
The common weasel for another ten hours /
Hitler allows no one to see him naked /
or in his bath /He's rumored to glow faintly
in shadow / Two shadows / Part of a dream is
still in the room / like a moth beating itself out
against the window / Embering / The sun is
cooling / cooling off / about 6,000 degrees now /
leaving the weasel's coat brown / though her face
stays totally white / This is when Hitler starts
his daily monologue /one of a litany that begins /
When I was in Vienna / When I was a soldier /
or When I was the leader in the early days
of the party / He talks for hours / Bored or
yearning / a Cro-Magnon woman makes paint
from her own blood / She draws a man
on the wall of a cave / names him a long noise /
Someone's in my apartment / using the sink /
I'm awake / the dream dead on the sill /
A thousand moths / a dozen cows / heaps
of bandaged cats / bring them to the tomb /
Do it now / And now / The Pharaoh must cross

the river of night / His slaves will follow /
The weasel is coming / into heat / She's so easy
to find / a Saxon calls her weosul—flowing /
Hitler spits coffee on a map of the world / does it
deliberately / whistling an American football song/
The continents break apart like cake / It's early /
It's late / It's a man in my kitchen / a stranger /
soap on his hands / face / Huge with strangeness /
Greta Garbo laughs in Hitler's private theater /
He makes Goebbles run the film until it scratches /
until the laugh becomes metal / Startled / two
weasels tumble a lantern / start the Chicago Fire /
The police blame a cow / Here they come / There
they go / Two deputies carry Hank Williams
to his limo / They bear him like a sack of rye /
hat on chest / Where are his boots / His God
damn guitar / He says / The window was open /
I just need to wash / Please don't call the cops /
Weasels are capable of many sounds / mostly
grunts / They can also scream / though rarely /
Only when fighting / Never in pain / Burning
they're quiet / The universe swells in total silence /
Above a whisper / Geronimo agrees to appear
in Buffalo Bill's Wild West Show / He tries hard
to keep quiet / keep it / but it gets away / History
is how quiet is lost / How it wanders / lives on
almost nothing / scraps / moths / follows the sun /
the seasons / the war / the carnival / Hitler loves
a traveling show / though he doesn't much care
for animal acts / unless there's a girl in danger /

The night at her back / a cavewoman makes a song /
the first song /out of old sighs / It draws a man
to her den / He lingers to hear it again / How do I
chase him away / When is the circus not in town /
the town not on fire / the hours bound for the dark /
I pour water / I open bread

Glossary

Deer in the headlights: to appear stunned,
lost for words, to "go blank"

Deer in the limelight: to walk on stage by
accident, to mark the audience, one hoof
raised

Deer in the searchlight: to be a mirror

Deer in the moonlight: to be half
remembered

Deer in the half-light: today we saw
the fawn, its shape against the lake,
falling from its mother's shape, as
she grazed ahead and it ran back
into her

Deer in the porch light: to wonder if
it's the same deer

Deer in the dear lights: in the dear, dear
lights

Deer in the candle, Northern, flood,
cave, dashboard, dawn's early light:
to be ruthlessly understood

Index of Titles and First Lines

Phase III

BEST CELLAR

A recent study has found that moths can summon memories from their lives as caterpillars, memories created prior to metamorphosis, the transitional stage during which their bodies and brains liquefy. There is currently no practical theory to explain this.

The Long While

We'd been sitting I don't know
how long, candles having that
effect on time, when you leant

across & said, What the country
needs is a servant class.
                    Words
that pushed me back in my seat.
No, you said, I mean an actual

class like a school, where we'd
all learn to serve. There'd be
whole semesters devoted to

waiting your turn or bowing or
scrubbing a patch of red carpet.
People would be graded on

not asking about their grades.
What do you think?
                    I thought
we'd been here quite a while
without seeing a menu. Then

I remembered how late it was,
we were in a barn, the table
between us a bed of straw.

The Needs of the Many

On the days when we wept—
and they were many—we did it
over the sound of a television
or radio, or the many engines
of the sky. It was rarely so quiet
we could hear just our sadness,
the smallness of it
that is merely the sound of wind
and water between the many pages
of the lungs. Many afternoons
we left the house still crying
and drove to a café or the movies,
or back to the hospital where we sat
dumb under the many eyes
of Paul Klee. There were many
umbrellas, days when it refused
to rain, cups of tea ignored. We
washed them all in the sink,
dry eyed. It's been a while,
we're cried out. We collect pauses
and have taken to reading actual
books again. We go through them
like yellow lights, like tunnels
or reunions, we forget which;
the older you are the more similes,
the more pangs per hour. Indeed,
this is how we break one hour into
many, how healing wounds time
in return. And though we know
there will always be crying to do,

just as there's always that song,
always a leaf somewhere in the car,
this may be the only sweetness left,
to have a few griefs we cherish
against the others, which are many.

STONEHENGE AT TWILIGHT

after William Turner of Oxford

From so far back, from this copper hour
when the flock comes muttering to drink,
how meager the stones appear, how like
a shepherd's teeth;
                              blue as the worm-
wood water, remote as the look in a cup.

Sheep don't see their reflections, don't
wonder at themselves, why their faces
aren't born away in a stream.
                              They say
their one vowel and remember the dog.

This far into evensong, how like a hand
the land seems, an open palm; the flock
but a strand of wool. As if the Lord
of shepherds were declaring,
                              Look,
what's in my purse instead of coins;
a bit of yarn to make more purses.

How like a smoking priest the distant
Heelstone seems, how like smoke
the curlews above it. They don't need
rods or tending.
                              They say their one say
and forget they said it.
                              So close to dark,
to campfires and propped sleep, yet still

within call of the sun, how like a field
is the sky, how much more like a herd
are the clouds than the birds.
                                    The stars
are a few songs away. Only a shepherd
would add them. Only a shepherd
wants to ask,
                        What man made those?
How did he put them there?

THE BEAR CHAPTER

No one watches the stewardess anymore;
how she demonstrates the belt, the mask,
the life vest. We've got it down. Maybe
not our lives, our money & regret, or how
to breathe while kissing, but, by God,
we know how to survive a water landing.
The stewardess doesn't look at us either,
but at someplace that's really behind her,
the way dancers do. It's a recital, after all.
In the wild we're told not to sleep too near
our food, to put even our champagne far
away. There's a checklist of other things,
written by a man so bored, he's forgotten
what survival is. Bears attack, he says,
if we surprise them. But he won't say
how; whether bears are easily frightened
or just don't like parties. When shipping
a bear by air, its ticket must be taped to
the cage in a waterproof bag. Someone
has to check this, someone who long ago
stopped imagining a sea full of floating
luggage, full of drowned bears in boxes.
The stewardess swims by. We call to her,
she to us; the ocean swallows our cries.
No surprises here.

Because You Watched
The Space Children

Because you watched *The Space Children*
we recommend *Aliens* and *The Man
From Planet X*. You might also consider
the Polish woman from next door, her
constant robe and flower pots. Other
picks include the boy who watched you
buy food at a gas station, the possum
on the roof, the word "helicopter." These
suggestions are based on your history.
You can always update your profile
by brooding at random: on your shoes,
a faraway chair, a blunder. Think of
things you could've said the last time
you fought with a lover. It was hard to
concentrate when your rockets failed;
the fire and sirens, the space children
locked arm in arm, ready to turn us all
to diamonds with a look.

Smiling Back

I remember when snowmen came right to our door
Some mornings it looked like a rally
You'd wake to a couple dozen, facing
the vague street, brooms & pitchforks raised high,
as if they expected some invading army

Back then you could still find emeralds
in pine cones; the grocer took them for cases of beer
His smile was like the spine of a leaf
I don't recall smiling back, I may not have
had a mouth, yet

Now everyone does; we all sputter like damp coal
& carry shovels to bed for protection
from whatever follows us to sleep

The Winds Now

blow the candles out in paintings,
they say, blow the wigs from old
statues. Wear layers, they say,
put on everything

you've got. I haven't seen that
sundress in years, the bouquets
of yellow on blue, frozen in free
fall. It used to be

all you wore. How strangely
it wears now, over six blouses,
three pairs of pants, & all your
stockings. Here comes

your good dress, followed by
the bad one, that "dirndl" thing,
a rain coat, a bigger coat,
& one, two, three,

seven hats. You'll want to sit
for the shoes, want to put your
hand on my shoulder. Let me do
the pushing, the tying;

focus on the window behind me.
Can you see the snow? Can you
see it going sideways? Pretend
you're on a train,

that you're riding it to town.
Pretend we have a town.

The Dreams of Trains

All day in the drag and clatter
of each other, the trains compass
their dreams. In their dreams

the trains lose their teeth, all
their tags; they go to Baltimore
naked. They have big parts

to play in a play about trains
but can't remember their lines:
New York/Los Angeles? Calcutta/

Bangalore? Everyone is staring
at them. They wish they could fly.
They can! But they can't look

down, because in their dreams
the trains are falling, falling
through tunnels of black smoke,

falling until shaken awake
by the bridges of Shanghai.

Fell Swoop

I killed a moth with a book
about the Johnstown flood. I broke
a window, too, the same window

where we watched the water stumble
down the street, then we climbed
out on the roof where we didn't have
a thing to read. The sky is so heavy,

so hard on a house like ours, it's all
I can do not to let the butterflies in
with a bit of sugar,
                a bit of talk
about candles, the garden we lost,
reading aloud from room to room.
Don't you ever want to crush a little

someone? Wonder if you hit me
hard enough, could we both leave
the ground?

ALL FATHERS EVE

Traditionally there's a dinner
served before dark. If you live
in town, traffic will be bad; up
country, the cows have made
an acre of corduroy, a dull
spell. All your people come,
people who share your father,
& they must bring excuses;
something like "The highway
is slow," or "The highway is
crazy," or "I wish they'd build
a highway." Inside you want
to have the TV going or music
a little loud. Your father isn't
visible at first; he can't appear
until everyone's there, until
the air is musked with bacon
& eggs & coffee, because dinner
is breakfast. He comes out then,
mid-sentence, telling the nearest
guest to turn off the damn TV
or whatever's making that noise.
How can anyone hear themselves
think. Yes, it's good to see you,
but let's sit down. He's so hungry
he could eat a horse, maybe two,
a year of horses, all the men
riding them, the cattle, the field,
the darkening shapes of women
on a hill.

En Route

I have a hard time with Hope,
with the "ope" sound of anything;

it tends to involve a lot of waiting.
Especially Dope.

Does a book of poems ever say,
I'll be with you right away?

Nope. It says, The bell tolls deep
in autumn's hinterland. I have

a hard time with that. Mostly I
have a hard time with "hinterland."

It means the land behind, which
is totally fine. But "hinterland"

sounds like a theme-park for
people who can't come to the point.

My point is that I have hard time
living with the unsolved: love,

the myth of money, those bells
that toll deep in my bed.

They're hopeless & that gives me
hope; unfounded, unreasonable,

uncapitalized hope I'll discover
or remember that the world isn't

the world, but a story of the world,
shared before we land.

Departing Gates

Describe one image from your first idea
of heaven / You were small / the size of
carry-on luggage / your dreams already
a travel risk / If this is a bad time / can
you name a good one / Can you say if
there were flowers / What about animals /

Start with the leopard / It was tame /
coaxed your hand into stroking / How
long did you meet its eyes / Now music /
It helps if you assign colors / Drums are
usually black / horns gold to orange /
It's alright if you need to cry / no

better time / really / You cry easier now /
don't you / That's not a real question /
We can stop / as soon as you address
the sky / an inch of sky / Make an inch
with your fingers and start talking / What
is the purpose for your stay

NIGHT STAND
for M.M.

We look at Mars, point at Mars, touch
Mars. You sing, Newton, Huygens, Laplace,
Kepler. I sing, Kingdom, Union, Chalice,
Scepter. You sing, Tycho Brahe. I shout,
He lost his nose in a duel! Got a new one
made of gold and silver! You sigh, Percival.

What of Percival Lowell? We feel bad for
not singing him. Between us we haven't
the heart. He was so sure about the men
and women of Mars, so sure they built
canals; and schools and armies and
an opera. If astronomy teaches anything,
he said, it's that we'll certainly meet
our cousins scattered throughout space.
We drink to Percival Lowell, we bow to
Percival Lowell, we dim the lights and kiss
but softly like neutrinos. It's too dark

to see the chart anymore. I sing Ptolomy,
Messier, Hawking and Hubble. I whisper
Galileo, Copernicus. You fumble the night-
stand for a candle, strike a match, pull me
down. This light, you say, has traveled
since the stars were in jail. It's come
all this way to crash with us.

The Last Superstition

I borrowed a book from a student, an encyclopedia
of superstitions. I promised to give it back today
but I can't. There's a robin outside, a crossed pair
of shoes in the corner. Don't get me started on how
bad this is; worse than keeping a dead man's keys.
Of course, I have to return it soon. My student just
turned fifteen, the age when we learn our parents are
damned. She's going to need answers, some code
to follow. The last superstition in the book comes
from 1640. Coincidentally it appears on page 164,
the left side, which means you really shouldn't read
this line: To regain youth, one must eat snakes.

The Man Who Did the Honors

assured us our dreams felt no pain.
They're way beyond that, he said,
and anyway I use logic instead
of the usual drugs. We weren't
sure what the usual drugs were.
And wouldn't dope be kinder
than reason, we wanted to ask.
Of course, it was his house, his
rules; the food excellent, the wine,
such nice things all around us.
We wanted to close our eyes,
to lose ourselves in the picture
we made. We tried. Nothing came.
You won't believe how well you sleep
tonight, he said, cleaning his spoon
with another spoon.

A Point of Losing

There's nothing of him
in his own room; a gallery
of his later years with no
exhibits, no catalogue,
touring all the same.

In his closet something
tolls, a chime when two
hangers touch: Last day,
last walk through.

Your father stands in
the bathroom door, light
pushing through his knees,
his faint arms, a scarecrow
for extended family.

It's his thing now, standing
like that, his last habit:
thresholding. He does it
in bed, too, grips the rails
on either side, ready
to board.

He made a point of losing,
he says, so he wouldn't need
to divvy. You sit at his side
with your sister, listening
as if a lamp had spoken.

I'm leaving you my luck,
he says, these old flowers,
and as much as I remember
of a woman who let me hold
her hip. You'll have to share.

Is Anyone Reading to You

(for Angelique L'Amour)

Is there a chair beside your bed / a plastic one where someone
reads a book / a newspaper / Can you even get a newspaper /
so deep in the building / Is there a TV / one that hangs
from the ceiling like a bird feeder / Do the nurses talk about
the world / Are they allowed /
                          Police in Connecticut have broken up
a canary-fighting ring / a den of men who gamble on one songbird
killing another / nineteen men who speak mostly Portuguese and won't
say how they got 100 birds to gladiate /
                          If you look up their word
for canary you find *canário* / Inexplicably / the phrases *Vinho
das canárias* and *Amarelo vivo* also appear / meaning *Wine
of canaries* and *Living yellow* / For me / it's the former /
that gives the greater pause / how it conjures barefoot women /
skirts hiked to their hips / dancing in a cask / treading birds
into bright water / Or maybe the birds do the dancing /

How long does it take animals who weigh little more
than sunlight to crush a cup of anything / Last night I went
dreaming and brought out two sentences /

              What is permanent falls asleep
              What is temporary wants to

Canaries are temporary / I think of you holding canaries to your chest /
a pair of tea cups / full of wild fruit / sun falling on a white iron
table / the music of oranges tumbling from a red knit bag / What
do you hear / Is there a radio / Do you get the classical station / any
piano / It helps healing / so I'm told / something about ivory and will /
Shostakovich claimed to hear music / new music / from a hunk
of shrapnel in his head / It poured out / faster than he could write /

day and night / flushing the wound with melody / Schumann suffered
a constant 'A' note / a side effect of the mercury he took for syphilis /
At first he couldn't compose in another key / but it grew / he said /
into heavenly trumpets / and voices / music bequeathed by ghosts /
by great composers /

They say canaries expand their brains
when singing / I'm not sure if this means their brains bloat with
the effort / or if their repertoires get bigger by the song / We do that /
too / At birth / the speech center is empty / As we gather words /
branches form / This is how language grows a tree in the brain /
a live oak with roots everywhere / warping the house / the sidewalk /
Would you believe when I was 12 years old / a doctor told me to
Just snap out of it?

For the 12 years Francois Beaugard
painted his nudes of Mary Magdelene / he agonized over how to hide
her breasts behind red canaries / It wasn't prudishness but his love
for Christ / a way to invoke the wounds of the prophet / which appear
in poems as nipples or springs where birds drink / No one cared /
He burned his paintings / then died singing / This is my song
of distraction / and I sing to you / Are you distracted / Try this /

Down by the shore an orchestra's playing
& even the palms seem to be swaying
when they begin . . .

A visiting hour never begins / or ends / It stays after everyone's gone /
pokes at your cup of soup / the lemon wedge / the humiliated flowers /
If I could be there I would read to you / I would empty the TV
over the sink / turn the sailboats to the wall / and read you the story
of the woman who put the birds to sleep by crossing her arms

STILL LIFE ON MARS

It's taken everything to bring them here:
the peaches, grapes, oysters, the goblet
of wine, the table & cloth. Hardest of all
was keeping the snail alive 300 days,
hearty enough to survive two seconds
of posing.
       We place it last, assuming the
other props will bear in the red air. They
don't. Before the snail dies (and it dies
in "One Mississippi") the peaches liquefy,
the grapes, too, the oysters implode like
novae. It's a massacre, right down to the
good linen & Château Latour.
               We paint it
anyway, going slow to compensate for
our ridiculous gloves, stiff necks, the dim
light of the afternoon which is blue here.
It's worth all this to get it right. Indeed,
our life has never been so urgently shown.
How brief the fruit, the vintage & vessel.
How apt the snail, the half inch
of its glittering service.

Notes

DEMENTIA, MY DARLING
The title of this poem comes from a musical composition by the great Frank Wess.

POEM MADE FROM LETTERS WRITTEN BY FRANCEYE
FrancEye aka Frances Dean Smith was an American poet. The lines of this poem are culled from seven different letters I received from her. I have changed only their order, not their content.

PEST IN BLUR
The title of this poem is an anagram for "Blueprint," the title of a drawing by artist Tyler Dow. The black & white image shows a large housefly baring an infant on its back.

EXAM
This poem was originally comissioned by Uninsured LA, a solidarity campagin in Los Angeles created to support health reform.

A FOUNDRY GONE
The title of this poem is an anagram of the phrase "For Dean Young."

Somniloquy
The title of this poem refers to the act of talking in one's sleep.

PHOTOTAXIS (No.3)
Many of the details concerning Adolph Hitler are taken from a report by the U.S. Office of Strategic Services (CIA), in December of 1942.

The Last Superstition
The book referred to in this poem actually exists. *The Encyclopedia of Superstitions* was compiled by Edwin and Mona Radford and published in 1949. You can still find it.

Stonehenge at Twilight
This poem was commissioned by WriteNow and The Getty Museum for their Dark Blushing project. It is a response to William Turner of Oxford's 1840 watercolor of the same name.

Afterword

This book would not be possible without Jayne Quackenbush. I'm likewise blessed beyond words for the love and wisdom of my mother and father, my sister and brother.

I'm also profoundly grateful to Sara Alexia, Cynthia Anderson, Khadija Anderson, Simone Beaubien, Sarah Benzel, J. Ryan Bermuda, Leslie Berry, Julie Bloemeke, J.J. Blumenkranz, Larry Bock, Conner Brenner, Lynne Bronstein, Derrick Brown, Shawn Burkley, Elena Karina Byrne, Jessica Ceballos, Alex Charalambides, Marcyn Del Clements, Billy Collins, Karen Cordova, Mark Cull, Amy E. Davis, Nicholas Earl Davis, Lea C. Deschenes, Natalie Diaz, Tracy Dillon, Alex Dimitrov, Michael Dobbs, Peggy Dobreer, Linda Dove, Alejandro Duarte, Mckendy Fils-Aime, Cinde Fincke, Janet Fitch, Meagan Ford, Lauren Elma Frament, Amelie Frank, Kate Gale, Lisa Gill, Dana Gioia, Gary Glazner, William Goldstein, Diana Gould, Moray Greenfield, S.A. Griffin, Gia Grillo, Stephanie Barbé Hammer, Daniel Handler, Jerri Hardesty, Kathleen T. Harris, Kodac Harrison, Marie Howe, Sandra Hunter, Elizabeth Iannaci, Victor Infante, Suzanne Isken, Katie Jacobs, William James, Erica W. Jamieson, Shaun Judah, Douglas Kearney, Jason Keller, Collin Kelley, Ross Kellogg, Shawnacy Kiker, Doug Knott, Paul Koenig, John Lacarbiere III, Marie Lecrivain, Amy Lemmon, Joe & Christina Liao, Suzanne Lummis, Rick Lupert, Kathleen Mackay, Amy Maclennan, Keith Martin, Paul Mathers, Daniel McGinn, Don McIver, Rachel McKibbens, Sam Mercer, Jeff Miller, Daryl Morazzini, Sean Patrick Mulroy, Erika Murray, Craig Nelson, Kate Noonan, Maureen O'Connell, the Oliva family (Hi, Erin!), Shawnte Orion, Judith Pacht, Lynn Pedersen, Alice Pero, Lynn O. Peterson, Christian Phiffer, Christopher & Angelique Pitney, William Plaschke, Lynne Procope, Jeremy Radin, Aaron Reeder, Tony de los Reyes, Cindy Rinne, Ann Leadingham-Seay, Sydney & Rosemary Sellers, Danielle Serio, Larisa Showalter, Adam Stone, John & Barbara St. Thomas, Rob Sturma,

Annette Sugden, Torene Svitil, Amber Tamblyn, Lynne Thompson, Vickie Trancho, Brian Turner, Diane Wakoski, Cynthia Waldman, Ilene Waterstone, Jon Wesick, Kristine Williams, Brandon Wilson, Mariano Zaro, Dana Zillgitt, and Adrian Todd Zuniga.

Biographical Note

Brendan Constantine's is work has appeared in *Field, Ploughshares, Virginia Quarterly Review, Prairie Schooner* and many other journals. He is the author of three previous collections: *Letters to Guns* (Red Hen Press, 2009), *Birthday Girl with Possum* (Write Bloody Publishing, 2011), and *Calamity Joe* (Red Hen Press, 2012). He has received grants and commissions from the Getty Museum, James Irvine Foundation, and the National Endowment for the Arts. A popular performer, Brendan has presented his work throughout the U.S. and Europe, also appearing on National Public Radio, numerous podcasts, and YouTube. He lives and teaches in Los Angeles.

Printed in the USA
CPSIA information can be obtained
at www.ICGtesting.com
JSHW080004150824
68134JS00021B/2263